Merry Christmas

Andrei

Xmas activity book

XmasSt

CONTENTS

Merry Christmas Andrei; I hope you enjoy this book. It is jam packed with cool stuff for you to do from crosswords, word searches, drawing and coloring.

It has loads of fun things for you to do over Christmas and the New Year.

Merry Christmas Andrei

FOR YOUR PARENTS

Thank you for buying this book, it will keep Andrei engaged over the Christmas Holidays and will help improve writing and math skills

It is also a good break from TV and computer games ☺

Keep it safe as it is a great keepsake of your child's early years

If you and Andrei like this book please leave us a review

We have lots of other personalized books to check out at:

www.XmasSt.com

Including:

Happy Birthday Andrei – The Big Birthday Activity Book

Happy Halloween Andrei – Spooky Activity Book

Happy Easter Andrei – Activity Book

And many more …

Merry Christmas Andrei

Your Name: Andrei

Age:

What you did over Christmas:

Where you went on Christmas Day:

Presents you got for Christmas:

Christmas Jokes

Christmas Jokes

What do snowmen eat for breakfast?
Snowflakes

What goes "oh, oh, oh?

Santa walking backwards

What is Father Christmas' wife called?

Mary Christmas

What do you get when you cross an archer with a gift-wrapper?

Ribbon hood

What do you call Santa Claus's dog?

Santa paws

What do snowmen wear on their heads?
Ice caps

Where do polar bears vote?
The North Poll

Why did the elf push his bed into the fireplace?
He wanted to sleep like a log

Why did the little girl change her mind about buying her grandmother a packet of handkerchiefs for Christmas?
She said "I could not work out what size her nose was

What goes in a chimney red and comes out of it black?
Santa Claus

What's white and red and goes up and down and up and down?

Santa Claus in an elevator

How do you scare a snowman?

You get a hairdryer

What do they sing under the ocean during the winter?

Christmas Corals

How much did Santa pay for his sleigh?

Nothing, it was on the house

What is invisible and smells like milk and cookies?

Santa's burps

What did the Gingerbread Man put on his bed?

A cookie sheet

What do you call a Santa that sleeps all the time?

Santa snores

What's a good holiday tip?

Never catch snowflakes with your tongue until all the birds have gone south for the winter

What does Santa clean his sleigh with?
Comet

What's black and white and red all over?
Santa covered with chimney soot

Why is Santa so good at karate?

Because he has a black belt

What's the best thing to give your parents for Christmas?
A list of everything you want

If athletes get athlete's foot, then what do astronauts get?
Missile-toe

What kind of bug hates Christmas?
A humbug

What two countries should the chef use when he's making
Christmas dinner?

Turkey and Greece

What did Mrs Claus say to Santa when she looked in the sky?
"Looks like rain, dear"

Why did Frosty have a carrot in his nose?

Because he forgot where the refrigerator was

What do vampires sing on New Year's Eve?

Auld Fang Syne

What did the Christmas tree say to the ornament?
"Aren't you tired of hanging around?"

What's Santa's favorite candy?

Jolly Ranchers

What did the reindeer say when he saw an elf?
Nothing, reindeer can't talk

What is big, red and flies in the sky?
Santa Clause

Which elf was the best singer?
ELFis Presley

How do you know when Santa's in the room?
You can sense his presents

What did the cow get for Christmas?

A COWculator

Knock knock
Who's there?
Irish
Irish who?
Irish you a Merry Christmas

What do elves learn at elf school?

The elf-abet

Knock knock.
Who's there?
Mary and Abbey
Mary and Abbey who?
Mary Christmas and Abbey New Year

What did one snowman say to the other snowman?

Can you smell carrot

What is Rudolph's favorite day of the year?

Red nose day

Why does Santa have a garden?

Because he likes to hoe hoe hoe

What's red and white and gives presents to good little fish at Christmas?

Sandy Claws

What do you say to Santa Claus when he is taking the register at school?

Present

What does Rudolph want for Christmas?

A snowy Sleigh-station

Where does Santa go to learn how to slide down chimneys?

The Chimnasium

Christmas Activities for Andrei

Word search, crossword and other fun activities

Answers are on the back of each puzzle page … no peeking

Big Xmas Word Search

Merry	Christmas	Andrei
Presents	Santa	Elf
Tinsel	Mistletoe	Snowman

X	T	U	B	G	O	I	E	R	D	N	A
F	N	A	M	W	O	N	S	Y	U	K	B
E	O	T	E	L	T	S	I	M	S	N	J
S	P	I	Y	N	N	J	V	A	A	S	Q
A	R	N	D	K	R	M	M	M	T	M	M
N	M	S	B	P	E	T	W	N	M	K	R
T	J	E	Z	R	S	T	E	L	F	T	Y
A	D	L	R	I	N	S	P	D	L	K	A
D	D	Y	R	S	E	P	J	Y	L	E	W
D	N	H	T	R	K	Q	Q	B	Y	B	I
V	C	W	P	R	Y	N	B	N	J	B	L
Y	U	L	E	T	I	D	E	V	D	H	N

There is one more, did you find it?

19

Big Xmas Word Search Answers

Merry	Christmas	Andrei
Presents	Santa	Elf
Tinsel	Mistletoe	Snowman

X	T	U	B	G	O	I	E	R	D	N	A
F	N	A	M	W	O	N	S	Y	U	K	B
E	O	T	E	L	T	S	I	M	S	N	J
S	P	I	Y	N	N	J	V	A	A	S	Q
A	R	N	D	K	R	M	M	M	T	M	M
N	M	S	B	P	E	T	W	N	M	K	R
T	J	E	Z	R	S	T	E	L	F	T	Y
A	D	L	R	I	N	S	P	D	L	K	A
D	D	Y	R	S	E	P	J	Y	L	E	W
D	N	H	T	R	K	Q	Q	B	Y	B	I
V	C	W	P	R	Y	N	B	N	J	B	L
Y	U	L	E	T	I	D	E	V	D	H	N

There is one more, did you find it?   Yuletide

20

Criss-Cross Crossword

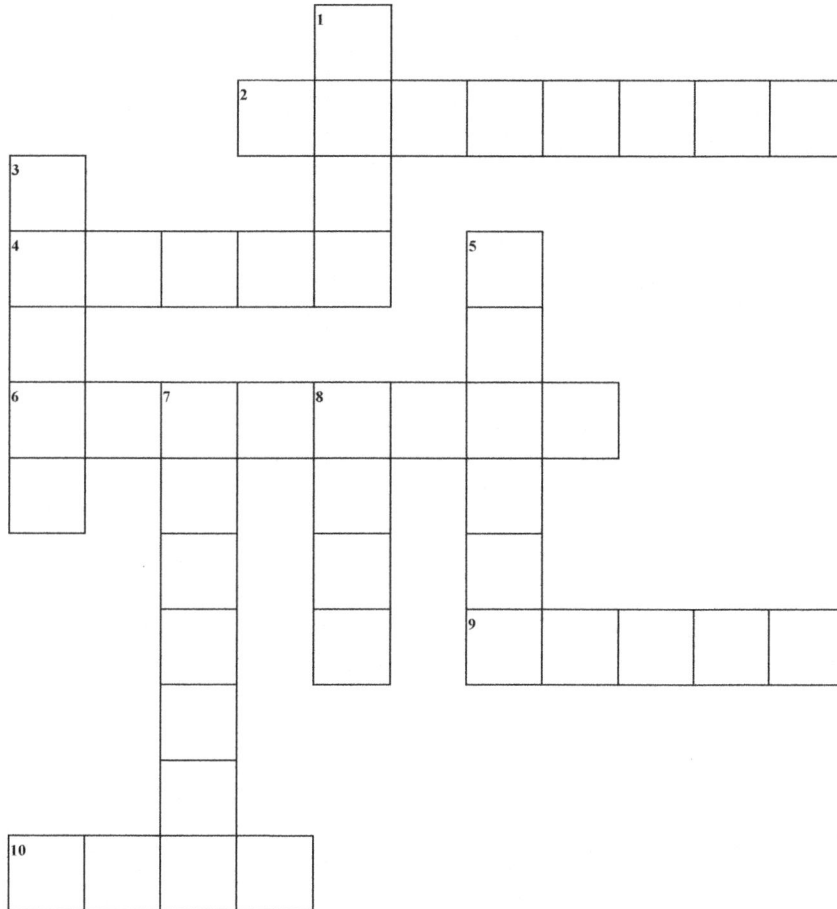

Across

2. What animals pull Santa's Sleigh
4. Put on top of a Christmas Tree
6. Month Christmas is in
9. Christmas plant and a girls name
10. You do this under Mistletoe

Down

1. Ornament on the tip of an Elf's shoe
3. You will get lots of these in the mail
5. What does Santa travel in

Snacks left out for Santa

7=Snack   8=Drink

21

Criss-Cross Crossword Answers

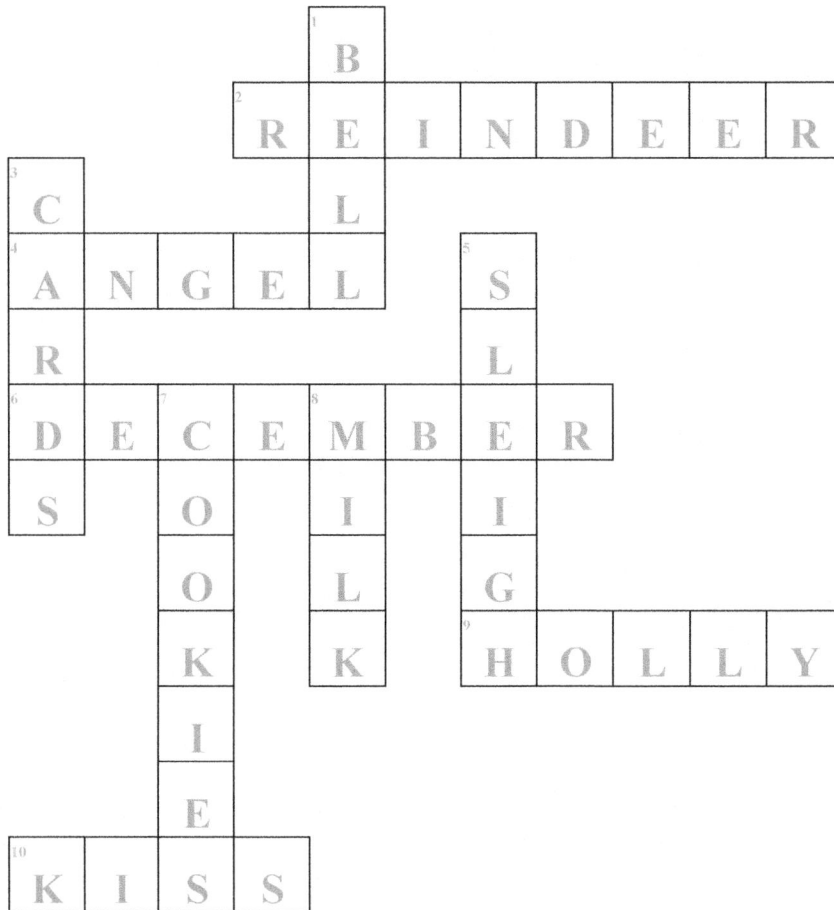

```
              B
        R E I N D E E R
        E
  C     L
  A N G E L       S
  R     L         L
  D E C E M B E R
  S     O     I   I
        O     L   G
        K     K   H O L L Y
        I
        E
K I S S
```

Across

2. What animals pull Santa's Sleigh
4. Put on top of a Christmas Tree
6. Month Christmas is in
9. Christmas plant and a girls name
10. You do this under Mistletoe

Down

1. Ornament on the tip of an Elf's shoe
3. You will get lots of these in the mail
5. What does Santa travel in
    Snacks left out for Santa
    7=Snack   8=Drink

Link Up Christmas

Link the letters, to make a word or phrase

CHRIS
TIN
TUR
PRE
SNO
DECOR
WRAP
AND
SURP
MIST

SENT
TMAS
WMAN
ATIONS
KEY
PING
RISE
LETOE
REI
SEL

Link Up Christmas Answers

Link the letters, to make a word or phrase

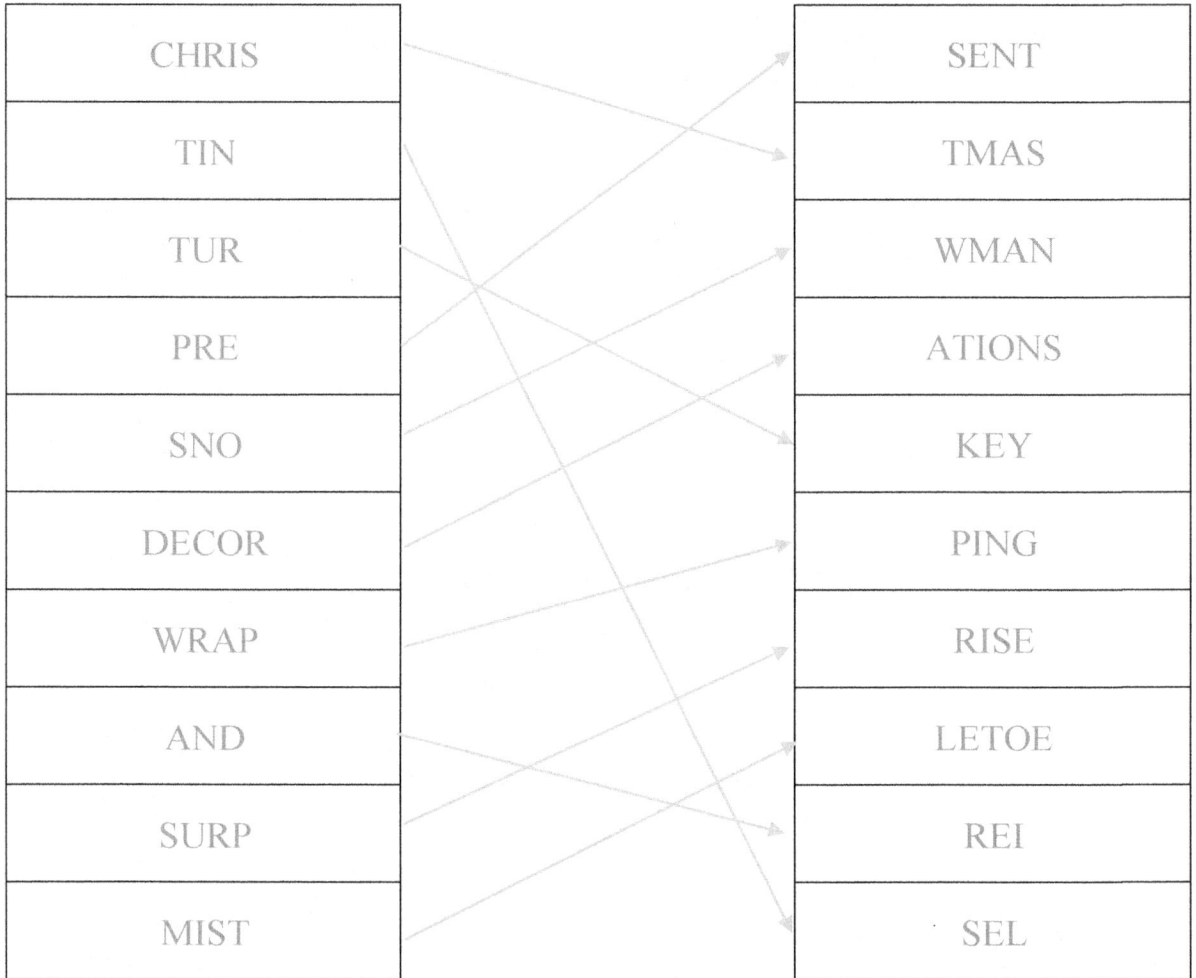

CHRIS	SENT
TIN	TMAS
TUR	WMAN
PRE	ATIONS
SNO	KEY
DECOR	PING
WRAP	RISE
AND	LETOE
SURP	REI
MIST	SEL

Santa Tile Mash Up

Rearrange the tiles to reveal the answer, write it below each one

Clue: Merry _____

ST	RI	AS	CH	M

_____

Clue: Santa lives there

LE	TH_	NOR	PO

_____

Clue: Your presents are covered by it

NG_	PPI	WRA	PER	PA

_____

Clue: You can build one out of snow

OW	N	A	M	SN

_____

Santa Tile Mash Up Answers

Rearrange the tiles to reveal the answer

Clue: Merry _____

ST	RI	AS	CH	M

MERRY CHRISTMAS

Clue: Santa lives there

LE	TH_	NOR	PO

NORTH POLE

Clue: Your presents are covered by it

NG_	PPI	WRA	PER	PA

WRAPPING PAPER

Clue: You can build one out of snow

OW	N	A	M	SN

SNOWMAN

The Fallen Message Puzzle

Each letter is in the correct column, but below where it should be.

Put the letters back in the grid to rebuild the secret message

		M		R		Y		
			I		T			

		A	E	D	T	E		
		R	N	S	R	Y	I	
C	H	M	I	R	R	M	A	S

The Fallen Message Puzzle Answer

Each letter is in the correct column, but below where it should be.
Put the letters back in the grid to rebuild the secret message

		M	E	R	R	Y		
C	H	R	I	S	T	M	A	S
		A	N	D	R	E	I	

		A	E	D	T	E		
		R	N	S	R	Y	I	
C	H	M	I	R	R	M	A	S

28

Rudolph's Secret Code

1. Solve the numbers puzzle

2. Convert the answer to a letter (1=A, 2=B, 3=C).
   Crack the secret code word.

				Number		Letter
20	-	2	=		=	
2	+	3	=		=	
19	-	10	=		=	
8	+	6	=		=	
15	-	11	=		=	
11	-	6	=		=	
7	-	2	=		=	
5	+	13	=		=	

Rudolph's Secret Code Answers

1. Solve the numbers puzzle

2. Convert the answer to a letter (1=A, 2=B, 3=C).
   Crack the secret code word.

				Number		Letter
20	-	2	=	18	=	R
2	+	3	=	5	=	E
19	-	10	=	9	=	I
8	+	6	=	14	=	N
15	-	11	=	4	=	D
11	-	6	=	5	=	E
7	-	2	=	5	=	E
5	+	13	=	18	=	R

Christmas Lights

1. Work out the math puzzle for each column below
2. Find the secret word, using the code (1=A, 2=B, 3=C)

10	16	19	4	8	12	9	18	6
+	+	-	-	+	+	-	-	+
6	4	6	2	7	6	4	7	12
=	=	=	=	=	=	=	=	=
-	-	+	+	-	-	+	+	-
8	12	2	9	11	16	12	4	9
=	=	=	=	=	=	=	=	=
-	-	+	-	+	+	-	-	+
6	3	5	3	8	3	9	10	4
=	=	=	=	=	=	=	=	=

Enter the letters above using the number code (1=A, 2=B, 3=C)

Christmas Lights Answers

3. Work out the math puzzle for each column below
4. Find the secret word, using the code (1=A, 2=B, 3=C)

10	16	19	4	8	12	9	18	6
+	+	-	-	+	+	-	-	+
6	4	6	2	7	6	4	7	12
=	=	=	=	=	=	=	=	=
16	**20**	**13**	**2**	**15**	**18**	**5**	**11**	**18**
-	-	+	+	-	-	+	+	-
8	12	2	9	11	16	12	4	9
=	=	=	=	=	=	=	=	=
8	**8**	**15**	**11**	**4**	**2**	**17**	**15**	**9**
-	-	+	-	+	+	-	-	+
6	3	5	3	8	3	9	10	4
=	=	=	=	=	=	=	=	=
2	**5**	**20**	**8**	**12**	**5**	**8**	**5**	**13**

B	E	T	H	L	E	H	E	M

Enter the letters above using the number code (1=A, 2=B, 3=C)

Christmas Cracker

Use the number codes to find the secret words

Tip (1=A, 2=B, 3=C) See page 124 to help, full list from A to Z

3	1	18	15	12	19

19	12	5	9	7	8

4	5	3	5	13	2	5	18

3	8	9	13	14	5	25

1	14	4	18	5	9

3	18	1	3	11	5	18	19

Christmas Cracker Answers

Use the number codes to find the secret words (Tip 1=A, 2=B, 3=C)

C	A	R	O	L	S

S	L	E	I	G	H

D	E	C	E	M	B	E	R

C	H	I	M	N	E	Y

A	N	D	R	E	I

C	R	A	C	K	E	R	S

Well done Andrei
Good job with the puzzles

Do you want some more puzzles?
Some drawing and coloring?

Coming up ...

Tinsel Tangler

Unscramble each of the anagram clue words; we will give you a clue with the two letters

Copy the letters in the numbered blocks to reveal the tinsel tangler words

MASCHRIST

C							S
	8				10		

LESNIT

T				L
	3			

DOLRUPH

	U		O		P	
6	11					

PRESTNES

P	R					T	S
			9				

IFGTS

	I		T	

1,4

DEERNIER

R							R

2

WBO

		W

7

RKTUEY

T			K		Y

5

Hidden Message

| 1 | 2 | 3 | 4 | 5 | 6 | 7 | 8 | 9 | 10 | 11 |

(Answers on the next page)

Tinsel Tangler Answers

Unscramble each of the anagram clue words; we will give you a clue with the two letters

Copy the letters in the numbered blocks to reveal the tinsel tangler words

MASCHRIST

C	H	R	I	S	T	M	A	S
	8					10		

LESNIT

T	I	N	S	E	L
	3				

DOLRUPH

R	U	D	O	L	P	H
6		11				

PRESTNES

P	R	E	S	E	N	T	S
				9			

IFGTS

G	I	F	T	S

1,4

DEERNIER

R	E	I	N	D	E	E	R

2

WBO

B	O	W

7

RKTUEY

T	U	R	K	E	Y

5

Hidden Message

G	I	N	G	E	R	B	R	E	A	D
1	2	3	4	5	6	7	8	9	10	11

Present Maze

Can you help Santa find his way through the maze to deliver the presents?

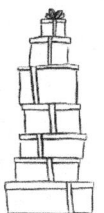

Reindeer Word Search

Dasher   **Dancer**   **Donner**

Blitzen   **Comet**   **Cupid**

Vixen   **Rudolph**   **Prancer**

X	D	N	G	C	E	Q	V	M	R	R	X
U	A	E	R	T	A	U	D	E	S	B	M
D	N	Z	B	S	O	A	H	F	B	W	C
M	C	T	E	Y	A	S	J	O	V	K	O
V	E	I	P	R	A	N	C	E	R	H	Q
N	R	L	G	D	J	D	S	D	P	I	D
E	S	B	J	Q	X	Y	I	L	P	O	K
X	P	D	H	Y	H	S	O	P	N	G	O
I	M	V	J	H	F	D	H	N	U	G	P
V	H	L	C	R	U	K	E	E	L	C	C
V	V	O	Y	R	D	R	R	F	R	T	P
U	R	J	A	T	E	M	O	C	V	R	C

Reindeer Word Search Answers

Dasher   Dancer   Donner

Blitzen   Comet   Cupid

Vixen   Rudolph   Prancer

X	D	N	G	C	E	Q	V	M	R	R	X
U	A	E	R	T	A	U	D	E	S	B	M
D	N	Z	B	S	O	A	H	F	B	W	C
M	C	T	E	Y	A	S	J	O	V	K	O
V	E	I	P	R	A	N	C	E	R	H	Q
N	R	L	G	D	J	D	S	D	P	I	D
E	S	B	J	Q	X	Y	I	L	P	O	K
X	P	D	H	Y	H	S	O	P	N	G	O
I	M	V	J	H	F	D	H	N	U	G	P
V	H	L	C	R	U	K	E	E	L	C	C
V	V	O	Y	R	D	R	R	F	R	T	P
U	R	J	A	T	E	M	O	C	V	R	C

What is my Present?

If you are completing the book before Christmas Day use the number codes below to find out what your main present is going to be

Tip (1=A, 2=B, 3=C) Look at the back page to help, full list from A to Z

25	15	21

23	9	12	12

8	1	22	5

20	15

23	1	9	20

20	9	12	12

3	8	18	9	19	20	13	1	19

4	1	25

1	14	4	18	5	9

What is my Present Answers

If you are completing the book before Christmas Day use the number codes below to find out what your main present is going to be

Tip (1=A, 2=B, 3=C) Look at the back page to help, full list from A to Z

Y	O	U

W	I	L	L

H	A	V	E

T	O

W	A	I	T

T	I	L	L

C	H	R	I	S	T	M	A	S

D	A	Y

A	N	D	R	E	I

Elf Code

1. Solve the numbers puzzle

2. Convert the answer to a letter (1=A, 2=B, 3=C). Crack the secret elf code

				Number		Letter
2	+	1	=		=	
5	+	3	=		=	
20	-	2	=		=	
12	-	3	=		=	
13	+	6	=		=	
14	+	6	=		=	
18	-	5	=		=	
8	-	7	=		=	
14	+	5	=		=	

Elf Code Answers

3. Solve the numbers puzzle

4. Convert the answer to a letter (1=A, 2=B, 3=C).
   Crack the secret elf code

				Number		Letter
2	+	1	=	3	=	C
5	+	3	=	8	=	H
20	-	2	=	18	=	R
12	-	3	=	9	=	I
13	+	6	=	19	=	S
14	+	6	=	20	=	T
18	-	5	=	13	=	M
8	-	7	=	1	=	A
14	+	5	=	19	=	S

Snowman Twister

1. Work out the math puzzle for each column below
2. Find the secret word, using the code (1=A, 2=B, 3=C)

9	8	7	6	5	4	3	2	1
+	+	+	+	+	+	+	+	+
9	8	7	6	5	4	3	2	9
=	=	=	=	=	=	=	=	=
-	-	-	-	-	-	-	-	-
4	6	8	10	6	7	4	3	2
=	=	=	=	=	=	=	=	=
+	+	+	+	+	+	-	+	-
5	4	9	21	2	11	1	10	3
=	=	=	=	=	=	=	=	=

Enter the letters above using the number code (1=A, 2=B, 3=C)

Snowman Twister Answers

3. Work out the math puzzle for each column below
4. Find the secret word, using the code (1=A, 2=B, 3=C)

9	8	7	6	5	4	3	2	1
+	+	+	+	+	+	+	+	+
9	8	7	6	5	4	3	2	9
=	=	=	=	=	=	=	=	=
18	**16**	**14**	**12**	**10**	**8**	**6**	**4**	**10**
-	-	-	-	-	-	-	-	-
4	6	8	10	6	7	4	3	2
=	=	=	=	=	=	=	=	=
14	**10**	**6**	**2**	**4**	**1**	**2**	**1**	**8**
+	+	+	+	+	+	-	+	-
5	4	9	21	2	11	1	10	3
=	=	=	=	=	=	=	=	=
19	**14**	**15**	**23**	**6**	**12**	**1**	**11**	**5**

S	N	O	W	F	L	A	K	E

Enter the letters above using the number code (1=A, 2=B, 3=C)

Christmas Brains

Name: **Andrei**

How many words to do with Christmas can you make

Complete against a friend (or your brother or sister)

Whoever has the most words will win

Tear these two pages out, so you can both complete it at the same time

Merry	Christmas	Santa

Christmas Brains

How many words to do with Christmas can you make

Complete against a friend (or your brother or sister)

Whoever has the most words will win

Tear these two pages out, so you can both complete it at the same time

Merry	Christmas	Santa

Decorate the Tree

Make you own Tree Decorations

1. Color the decorations
2. Cut them out carefully
3. Add string
4. Hang them on your Christmas Tree

Draw your favorite Present

My present is: _____

We wish you a Merry Christmas

& Happy New Year Andrei

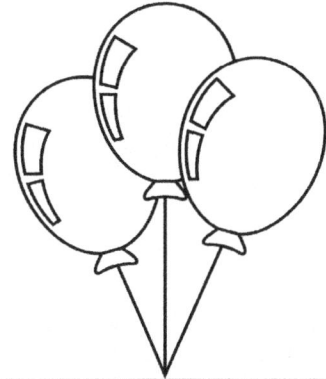

Don't forget to
thank your
Parents

On the next page you can write them a letter, fill in the blanks, tear
it out carefully and surprise them

Dear _____

Thank you so much for a great Christmas, I had a
great time at

_____

Thank you for all my amazing presents, some of
my favorite presents are

_____

_____

_____

Love

_____

Andrei   xxx

—

Decorate your own Christmas Banner

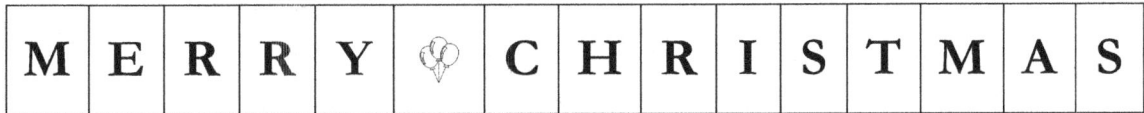

M	E	R	R	Y		C	H	R	I	S	T	M	A	S

Instructions:

1. Color and decorate each letter on each page

2. Cut each page out carefully

3. Stick them together side by side

The final sign will say

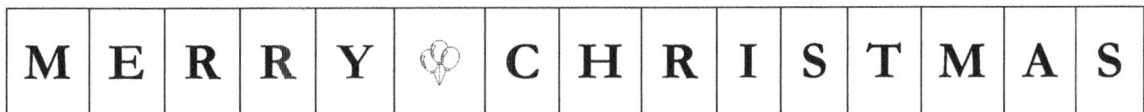

M	E	R	R	Y		C	H	R	I	S	T	M	A	S

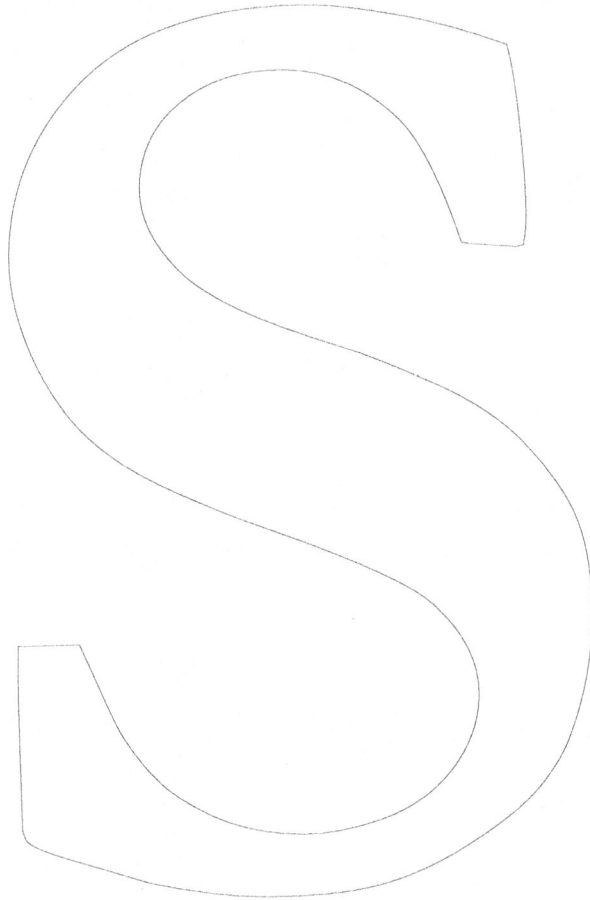

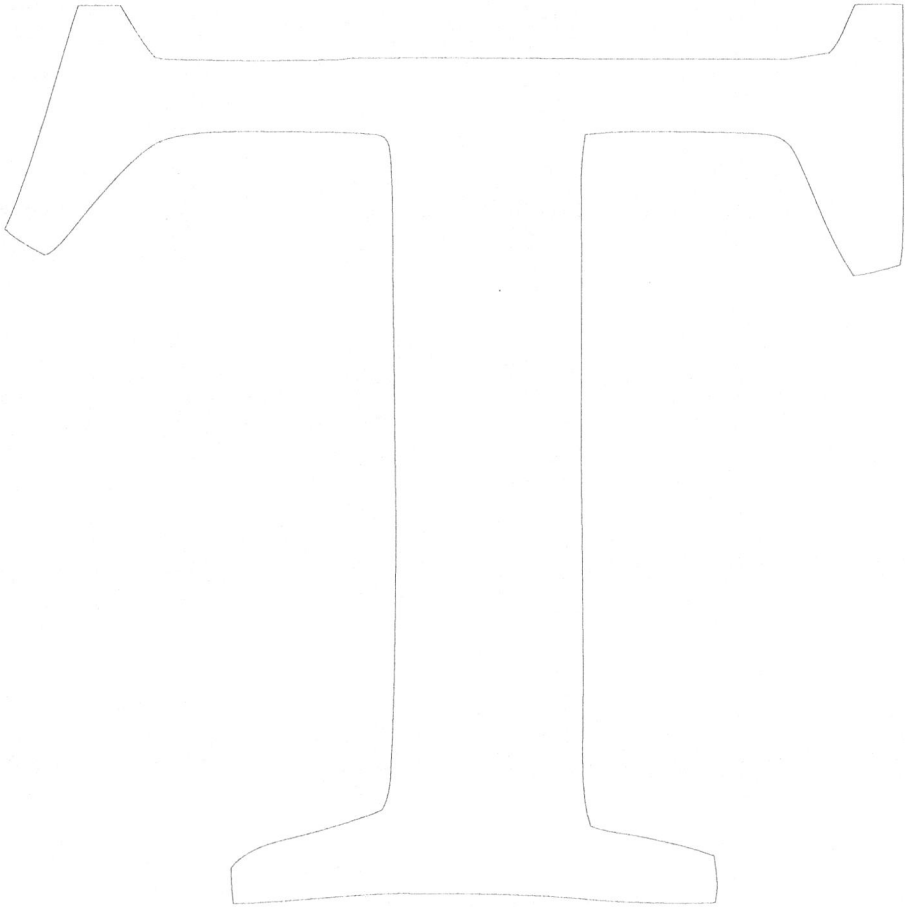

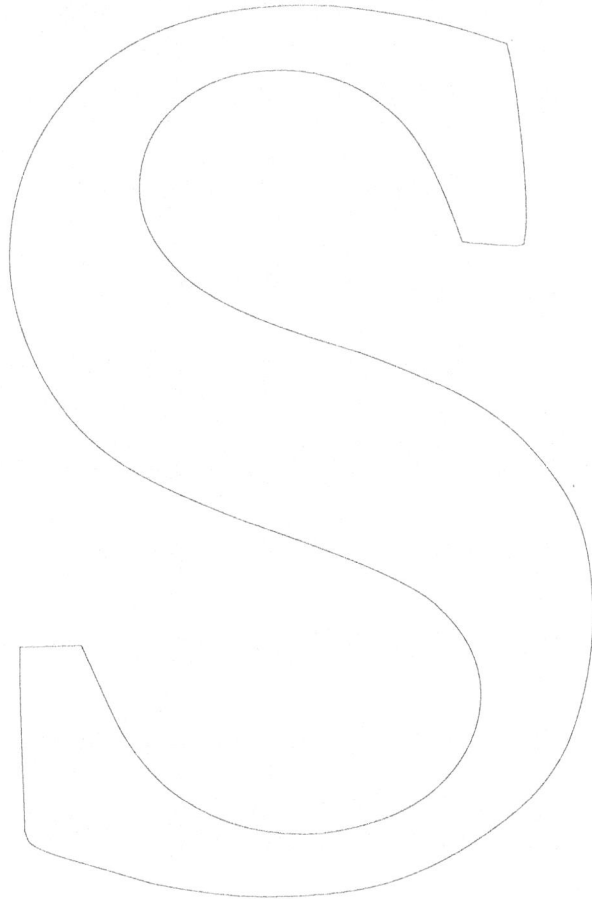

More Cool Christmas Jokes

What do you get when you cross a snowman with a vampire?

Frostbite

What's brown and sneaks round the kitchen?

Mince spies

What is the difference between the Christmas alphabet and the ordinary alphabet?

The Christmas Alphabet has Noel (No L)

What is all mum's favorite Christmas carol?

Silent night

What do you call people who are afraid of Santa Claus?
Claustrophobic

What do you call Santa when he stops moving?
Santa Pause

Where does a snowman keep his money?
In a snow bank

Why do mummies like Christmas so much?
Because of all the wrapping

What do you get if you eat Christmas decorations?

Tinsel-itus

What goes red white red white red white?

Santa rolling down a hill

What does Father Christmas always go down the chimney?

Because it soots him

Why did Santa Claus take his Christmas tree to the dentist?

To get a root canal

Why did the gingerbread man go to the doctor?
He was feeling crummy

Why does Scrooge love Rudolph the Red-Nosed Reindeer?

Because every buck is dear to him

Why is it so cold on Christmas?
Because it's in Decemberrrrr

What is Santa's favorite American state?
Idaho-ho-ho

What would you get if you crossed Santa with a giraffe?

St. Neck

What do you call a letter sent up the chimney on Christmas Eve?

Black mail

What would a reindeer do if it lost its tail?

She'd go to a "re-tail" shop for a new one

How did the chickens dance at the Christmas party?

Chick to chick

What beats his chest and swings from Christmas cake to Christmas cake?

Tarzipan

Mum, Can I have a dog for Christmas?

No you can have turkey like everyone else

What do Eskimos sing when they get their Christmas dinner?

"Whale meat again, don't know where, don't know when"

What do vampires put on their turkey at Christmas?
Grave-y

Do policeman eat turkey for Christmas?
No, they eat truncheon meat

What did the grape say to the peanut butter?
"'Tis the season to be jelly"

What do ducks do before Christmas dinner?
Pull their Christmas quackers

What do elves say when they meet each other?
Small world, isn't it?

How do you describe a rich elf?
Welfy

How many elves does it take to change a light bulb?
Ten. One to change the light bulb and nine to stand on each other's shoulders

If there were 11 elves, and another one came along, what would he be?
The twelf

Santa rides in a sleigh. What do elves ride in?
Mini vans

What do Elves use to go from floor to floor?
An Elfevator

What is a female elf called?
A shelf

What kind of money do elves use?
Jingle bills

Why did the elves ask the turkey to join the band?
Because he had the drum sticks

Why does Santa owe everything to the elves?
Because he is an elf-made man

How do we know Santa is such a good race car driver?
Because he's always in pole position

How does Santa take his photos?
With his North Pole-aroid camera

How many chimneys does Santa go down?
Stacks

Twinkle, Twinkle chocolate bar
Santa drives a rusty car
Press the starter
Press the choke
Off he goes in a cloud of smoke

What do you call a smelly Santa?
Farta Christmas

What do you call Father Christmas after he has come down the
chimney?
Cinder Claus

What do you call Santa when he has no money?
Saint "Nickel-less"

What do you get if you cross Santa with a flying saucer?
A UF ho, ho, ho

What does Santa Claus do when his elves misbehave?
He gives them the sack

What does Santa use when he goes fishing?
His north pole

What kind of motorcycle does Santa ride?
A "Holly" Davison

What smells most in a chimney?
Santa's nose

What sort of phone has Santa got?
Pay as you ho, ho, ho

Where does Santa stay when he's on holidays?
At a Ho-ho-tel

What comes at the end of Christmas Day?
The letter "Y"

What did one Christmas light say to the other Christmas light?
You light me up

What do Eskimos use to hold their homes together?
Ig-glue

What's Tarzan's favorite Christmas song?
Jungle bells
But what about his chimp?
King Kong merrily on high, of course

Where does mistletoe go to become famous?
Holly-wood

What did one Christmas tree say to the other?
I've got a present fir you

What did the dog get for Christmas?
A mobile bone

Did Rudolph go to a regular school?
No, he was elf-taught

Father Christmas has two reindeer. He calls one Edward and the other one Edward

I bet you can't tell me why he does that

"Oh, yes I can" the elf said

"Because two Ed's are better than one"

How does Rudolph know when Christmas is coming?
He looks at his calen-deer

What do you call the reindeer with one eye higher than the other?
Isaiah

What do you give a reindeer with an upset tummy?
Elk-a-seltzer

What does Father Christmas call that reindeer with no eyes?
No-eye-deer

What does Father Christmas call his three legged reindeer?
Eileen

What has antlers and loves cheese?
Mickey Moose

What reindeer can jump higher than a house?
They all can, houses can't jump

What's the name of the reindeer with three humps on its back?
Humphrey

Which of Santa's reindeer has bad manners?
Rude-olph

Why don't Prancer and Dancer and the other reindeer overtake
Rudolph?
Because they don't believe in passing the buck

What's a barber's favorite Christmas song?
'Oh comb all ye faithful'

What do you call Frosty the Snowman in May?
A puddle

Who looks after Father Christmas when he's ill?

The National Elf Service

Where do reindeer go to dance?
Christmas balls

What did the cow say on Christmas morning?

Mooey Christmas

What's red, white and blue at Christmas time?
A sad candy cane

What do you give a railway station master for Christmas?

Platform Shoes

What is the best Christmas present in the world?

A broken drum, you can't beat it

How do you make opening your Christmas presents last longer?

Open them with boxing gloves on

What do you call a man who claps at Christmas

Santapplause

Who gives presents to baby sharks at Christmas?

Santa Jaws

What did Adam say on the day before Christmas?

It's Christmas, Eve

What do you have in December that you don't have in any other month?

The letter D

Why is it difficult to keep a secret at the North Pole?

Because your teeth chatter

What does Santa Claus' cat want for Christmas?

Some new Clause

Where does Santa's little helpers go to relax?

The Elf Farm

What do you get if you cross Santa Claus with a duck?

Christmas Quackers

What did the snowman order at McDonalds?

Iceberg-ers and chilli sauce

What do you call a snowman on rollerblades?

A snow mobile

How can a snowman lose weight?

He waits till it gets warmer

What often falls at the North Pole but never gets hurt?

Snow

Knock, knock

Who's there?
Snow
Snow who?
Snow business like show business

What's white and goes up?

A confused snowflake

What is the best thing to put into a Christmas Cake?

Your teeth

What did one Christmas cracker say to the other Christmas cracker?

My Pop is bigger than yours

What do reindeer hang on their Christmas trees?
Horn-aments

What did Cinderella say when her photos didn't arrive on time?

One day my prints will come

What happened to the man who stole an advent calendar?

He got 25 days

What do witches use to wrap their presents?

Spello-tape

Why couldn't the skeleton go to the Christmas party?

He had no body to go with

What do you call an old snowman?
Water

What do you sing at a snowman's birthday party?

Freeze a jolly good fellow

What do snowmen like to do on the weekend?
Chill out

What does Jack Frost like best about school?
Snow and tell

What do you get if you cross an iPad with a Christmas tree?
A pineapple

What do elves do after school?
Their gnome work

What's the difference between Santa's reindeer and a knight?
One slays the dragon, and the other's draggin' the sleigh

Darth Vader: I know what you're getting for Christmas

Luke: How do you know?

Darth Vader: I can feel your presents

How does a sheep say Merry Christmas?

"Fleece Navidad"

What did the sheep say to the shepherd at Christmas?

Seasons Bleatings

What happens when Frosty the Snowman gets dandruff?
He gets snowflakes

Knock knock
Who's there?
Snow
Snow who?
Snow use, I've forgotten my name again

When does Christmas come before Thanksgiving?

In the dictionary

What do you call an elf who sings?

A wrapper

What do angry mice send to each other at Christmas?

Cross mouse cards

What game do reindeer play in their stalls?
Stable-tennis

What do you get if you cross Santa Claus with a detective?
Santa Clues

What do you get if Santa goes down the chimney when the fire is lit?
Crisp Cringle

How do sheep greet each other at Christmas?
A merry Christmas to ewe

Why are Christmas trees like bad knitters?
They both drop needles

How does Jack Frost get to work?

By icicle

Father Christmas' sledge broke down on Christmas Eve. He flagged down a passing motorist and asked, 'Can you help me fix my sledge?'
'Sorry,' the motorist replied. 'I'm not a mechanic - I'm a chiropodist.'
'Well, can you give me a toe?'

What do you call a bunch of chess grandmasters bragging about their games in a hotel lobby?

Chess nuts boasting in an open foyer!

Last year, I asked Santa for the smartest person ever for Christmas

I woke up in a box

There was once a great King in Russia named **Rudolph the Red**. He stood looking out the windows of his palace one day while his wife, the queen sat nearby knitting.

He turned to her
and said, "Look my dear, it has begun to rain!" Without even looking up from her knitting she replied, "It's too cold to rain. It must be sleeting.

The King shook his head and said, "I am the King, and Rudolph the Red knows rain, dear!"

Have a great Christmas

ANDREI

If you liked this book please leave us a review

We have lots of other personalized books to check out at:

www.XmasSt.com

Including:

Happy Birthday Andrei – The Big Birthday Activity Book

Happy Halloween Andrei – Spooky Activity Book

Happy Easter Andrei – Activity Book

And many more ...

  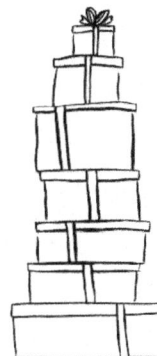

Number Codes

1 = A
2 = B
3 = C
4 = D
5 = E
6 = F
7 = G
8 = H
9 = I
10 = J
11 = K
12 = L
13 = M
14 = N
15 = O
16 = P
17 = Q
18 = R
19 = S
20 = T
21 = U
22 = V
23 = W
24 = X
25 = Y
26 = Z

Made in the USA
Las Vegas, NV
21 December 2021